Vladimir Antonov

Patanjali's

Ashtanga Yoga:

from Theory —
to Practical Realization

Translated from Russian
by Mikhail Nikolenko
and Maxim Shafeyev

Corrector of an English translation —
Keenan Murphy

2008

ISBN 978-1438200316

In ancient times, Indian rishi Patanjali highlighted the principal stages of the ascent to spiritual heights, to the Primordial Consciousness.

He distinguished eight major steps of this ascent: yama — niyama — asana — pranayama — pratya-hara — dharana — dhyana — samadhi.

Let us look at these steps.

Contents

www. philosophy-of-religion.org.ua
www.highest-yoga.info
www.swami-center.org

Yama and Niyama

These terms are translated as "effort and re-laxation" or "exertion and rest". This stage consists in mastering fundamental ethical and psycho-hygienic rules of the spiritual seeker's life.

The first rule is called ahimsa — non-harm-ing. It means trying not to injure, as far as possible, any living being in deeds, words, thoughts or emotions.

This also includes the principles of ethically correct nutrition that we have discussed in [4] and, what is no less important, getting rid of coarse emotions, which are the result of ill thoughts and often provoke rude words and actions.

We can make ethical mistakes, including crimes, as a result of either our ignorance, lack of understanding of the universal order and of our place and role in it, or as a result of our indulg-ing in the emotions of spite, condemnation, jeal-ousy, resentment, anxiety, despair, fear, etc, which are manifestations of the "sticking out" lower "I" (lower self).

Destroying the lower "I" by merging it into the universal Higher "I" of the Creator is one of the important tasks on the spiritual Path. This kind of work begins with the inner fight against all vicious manifestations of the lower "I" — first of all, those existing in the field of emotional reactions.

Repentance is an important tool in accomplishing this task — sincere repentance for ethical mistakes that one has committed, accompanied by a mental analysis of the corresponding problematic situations and finding the best ways of resolving them.

Many people do not grasp the essence of the principle of non-condemnation. Condemnation is an emotion, a form of anger. Identification and discussion of one's mistakes, as well as an intellectual analysis of them are not condemnation at all. An analysis is necessary since it helps us not to repeat someone else's mistakes. But while performing this type of analysis, one should be free from any kind of the emotions of anger.

Emotions are states of the energy of the consciousness. They emanate beyond the body, thus creating energy environment for people and other beings around us. People living in coarse emotional states produce a destructive and pathogenic environment for those around them. Communicating with such people can cause severe energy lesions and diseases, especially in children.

But people who live in subtle states of love make everything around their bodies healthy, spiritualized, and elevated; they heal with their mere presence. And the stronger their love and more powerful the consciousness is — the larger space they spiritualize — up to the planetary scale.

A spiritual seeker can achieve full control over the emotional sphere only through working with the chakras and other energy structures and then through merging (as a consciousness) with the Divine Consciousness. But he or she should start making efforts right from the beginning of the Path.

The second rule of yama is sathya — truthfulness, purity, honesty.

However, there are cases when we cannot tell the truth, because this will harm someone. In such instances it is better to evade answering the question...

But if we lie, we become sinners before God and captives to our lies before people, since we will have to apprehend a disclosure and to live in anxiety, instead of the state of steadfast pure peace.

The third rule is asteya — non-covetousness, renunciation of the desire to possess something that belongs to someone else. We have to be totally concentrated on the cognition of God! Craving for material objects, especially those belonging to others, is an utter perversion of the true orientation of the consciousness, which at the same time results in harming other people.

The fourth rule is aparigraha — limiting possessions to necessary things. Unnecessary things only distract our attention from the essential: from aspiration for Mergence with the Creator.

Brahmacharya — the fifth rule — literally means "walking the path of Brahman (Holy Spirit)". This implies renunciation of earthly desires (except for attending to the basic needs of the body) and redirection of the attention towards God, searching for Him first with the mind and then — with the developed consciousness.

This rule implies sincere renunciation of seeking earthly fame and honors, of accumulating the things that are unnecessary on the spiritual Path, and renunciation of the embellishment of the body.

Some people interpret the Brahmacharya rule only as celibacy (sexual abstinence). But this is too narrow of an interpretation. Besides that, sexual continence is unnecessary provided that one regards sex as a spiritual act. On the contrary, celibacy can result in adenoma of prostate in men, in energetic "fading" of women, and in the consciousness growing "callous" — in both. It really does not contribute to one's progress on the spiritual Path. What is important is not abstaining from sex, but freeing oneself from being obsessed with it and from sexual contacts with inadequate partners.

The sixth rule is saucha — maintaining purity of the body. The main thing here is to wash the whole body with warm or hot water and with soap, daily if possible. This cleans the skin from deposits of perspiration salts, which upset the normal functioning of the whole organism. Let us recall what we feel after taking a good bath, especially if we have not washed the body for a long time! This is the state of comfort that we can and should create for ourselves every day by washing the body in the morning.

Saucha also implies brushing the teeth and so on.

There are also special therapeutic saucha techniques, such as abstersion of the nose and of the nasopharynx by drawing in salted water. There is no reason for using them regularly, but they can be effective for treating chronic rhinitis.[1]

The seventh rule is mitahara — pure nutrition. This has already been discussed in detail in [4]. Here let me mention only that it is best to take food in an emotionally favorable environment.

---

[1] See more details in [4].

In no circumstances should one eat on the background of conflict conversations or bitter arguments, as well as in presence of malicious or irritated people.

One may perform a meditation before taking a meal in order to harmonize the inner state.

For example, the Orthodox prayer-meditation *Heavenly Father* suits this purpose very well.

The eighth rule — santosha — consists in maintaining a positive emotional attitude always. If we feel the presence of the Lord and devote our lives to Him totally, if we do not act out of self-interest, if we know that He is constantly watching us, leading us, teaching us, that He creates difficulties for us so that we can learn and then helps us find solutions to the problems — why would we not live in joy?

"You do your work; I control the events," — this is what He taught the author of this book once [10].

The ninth rule is svadhyana — philosophical discussions, conversations, and readings that make for a thorough comprehension of the meaning of life and of the Path to Perfection.

"Fix your mind on Me..." — this is how Krishna defined the first steps that man has to take on the Path to God [3].

The tenth rule — tapas — implies any kinds of self-restraint and efforts for the sake of overcoming our vices. Among other things, tapas teaches us the spiritual discipline as well as to follow the principle "it must be done!" as opposed to "I do only what I want!".

The eleventh rule is Ishvarapranidhana. This implies feeling that everything existing is pervaded with the Consciousness of the Creator (Ishvara), feeling His constant presence inside and outside my body, bodies of other people and material objects, seeing Him as my Teacher and a Witness of everything that I do and that happens to me.

There are also four very important rules:

— kshama — tolerance to those who think differently;

— daya — mercy, kindness;

— arjava — simplicity, absence of arrogance;

— hri — lowliness of mind, also absence of: self-admiration, self-pride because of one's actual achievements, and conceit — self-praise on account of one's imaginary virtues.

Asana

In this context, the word *asana* means a posture, a steady position of the body. There are special methods of working with the body in order to prepare it for further stages of spiritual work.

Systems of asanas and other exercises of this stage of work are collectively called Hatha Yoga. They also help one acquire the initial skills of concentration and provide the entry-level development of the energy structures of the organism.

One should start doing asanas only after studying and accepting the principles of the previous stage. Practicing Hatha Yoga without switching to the *killing-free diet*[2] results in coarsening of one's energy and in accumulation of coarse power, and this, in turn, makes one go astray from the true Path.

The best time for doing asanas is early morning — approximately 4-5 a.m.

Each session must be followed by shavasana — a deep relaxation of the body and mind while lying on the back for about 20 minutes. If one does not do this, health disorders may occur, such as deterioration of the eyesight, anxiety, insomnia, etc.

Attempts to do anything with Kundalini as a part of Hatha Yoga training are strictly prohibited: this can result in severe health disorders — both physical and mental. Working with Kundalini is a task of the Buddhi Yoga stage. Raising Kundalini is allowed only after all the chakras and major meridians have been cleansed and developed thoroughly.

---

[2] I.e. that which excludes bodies of killed animals.

One also needs to understand that Hatha Yoga is just a preparatory stage for the actual Yoga Path. This is why dedicating one's life to it, counting on any substantial spiritual success — is not serious. Only working with the spiritual heart within raja and then Buddhi Yoga programs can ensure serious advancement.

Pranayama

Working with energies within the body and within the *cocoon* that surrounds the body is the task of Raja Yoga. One of the methods here is pranayama, which is translated as "work with energy".

Sometimes this term is incorrectly interpreted as "breathing exercises". This is an atheistic error. In reality it is the energy of the consciousness that gets moving during pranayamas, but one may perform this — for convenience — keeping time with the breath.

The part of the consciousness that is working during pranayamas has to transform itself into white flowing *light*. With this *light*, we wash all areas of bio-energetic contamination located within our bodies. It results in general improvement of the health and elimination of various diseases. Also the consciousness itself turns into a mobile and active power.

Pratyahara

The word *pratyahara* means "removing the indriyas from material objects". At the stage of pratyahara, aspirants learn to control the "tentacles" of the consciousness which are called *indriyas* in Sanskrit. This allows one to achieve the ability to see in subtle and the subtlest layers of multidimensional space, as well as to exit from the material body into them and settle in them, accustoming oneself to their subtlety, tenderness, and purity.

The concept of indriyas exists only in the Indian spiritual culture. Europeans with their simplified and degraded religious ideas usually are not capable of grasping this kind of knowledge. Even in translations from the Indian languages they substitute the word *indriyas* with the word *senses*; by doing this they completely reject the immense methodological significance of pratyahara concept and of the principles of work at this stage.

Europeans translate the term *pratyahara* as "control over the senses". But senses are not everything that is denoted by the term indriyas, since the indriyas include the mind as well. It is also essential that the image of "tentacles" evoked by the word *indriyas* provides profound understanding of the principles of functioning of the mind and consciousness, as well as of methods of controlling them.

Krishna presented fundamental knowledge about working with the indriyas in the Bhagavad Gita [3]. He was talking about the indriyas of vision, audition, smell, touch, proprioception, and about those of the mind. And indeed: one's concentration on an object through any organ of sense or with the mind is very similar to extending a tentacle to it from the body. When one switches the concentration to another object, one detaches and moves the indriyas to it.

In the same manner the mind creates its own indriyas, when one thinks about something or someone.

People with developed sensitivity can perceive other people's indriyas touching them. In some cases they can even see those indriyas and therefore can influence them.

Krishna said that one of the things man has to learn is the ability to draw all the indriyas from the material world inwards, just as a tortoise retracts its paws and head into its shell. Then one has to extend the indriyas into the Divine eons in order to embrace God with them, to draw oneself to Him, and to merge with Him.

Now Sathya Sai Baba — our contemporary Messiah — also teaches about control over the indriyas. Many of His books have been translated into Russian but in all of them the information about working with the indriyas was lost due to inadequate translation.

One cannot achieve control over the indriyas without mastering the ability to shift the concentration of the consciousness between the chakras and main meridians, i.e. the meridians that make up the *microcosmic orbit* and the middle meridian. We have described in detail the methods of working with the chakras and meridians and the use of *places of power* for this — in the book [4].

Dharana

Dharana means "maintaining a proper concentration". Proper concentration means keeping the indriyas on God. In other words, this is a real manifestation of our aspiration for God, for Mergence with Him.

But God in the aspect of the Creator or the Holy Spirit is inaccessible for direct perception at this stage of apprenticeship.

Our loving thirst for God can be partially quenched by working with an Image of a Divine Teacher, for example, Jesus Christ, Babaji, or Sathya Sai Baba — the One Whose form from His past Incarnation is familiar to us.

If we hold such an Image in anahata on the background of the emotion of the most intense love that we are capable of, we gradually enter the state when it is not I who look at the world from anahata but He. This denotes the Yidam (this is what this Image is called) becoming alive; we are partially merged with Him. After that we may live in Unity with Him in anahata; having moved the concentration of the consciousness to the chakras located in the head, we can address Him in anahata as an Advisor and a Teacher.

This is not an illusion but the real Divine Teacher entering into His Image created by us. He may also become an Instructor in our meditative trainings. He will lead His devoted and loving disciples through Himself — into the Abode of the Creator.

"If you can visualize the Image of the Teacher in your consciousness with the most complete clarity, you can transfer your consciousness into His, and thus act through His Power, as it were. But for this, you must visualize the Image of the Teacher with utmost precision, to the minutest detail, so that the Image does not flicker, suffer distortion or change Its outlines, as it frequently happens. But if following the exercise of concentration one succeeds in invoking the steady Image of the Teacher, through this one may gain the greatest benefit for oneself, for those around one, and for the work." [1]

"You may be asked how the entrance upon the path of Service is defined. Certainly, the first sign will be renunciation of the past and total aspiring towards the future. The second sign will be realization of the Teacher within the heart not because it is one's "duty", but because it is impossible otherwise. The third sign will be rejection of fear, for the one who is armed by the Lord is invulnerable. The fourth will be non-condemnation, because the one who strives into the future has no time to occupy oneself with the refuse of yesterday. The fifth will be the filling of the entire time with labor for the future. The sixth will be the joy of Service and completely offering oneself for the good of the world. The seventh will be spiritual aspiration for the far-off worlds as a predestined path. According to these signs you will discern warriors that are ready and manifested for Service. They will understand where to raise the sword for the Lord, and their words will be from the heart." [1]

If work with Yidam does not bring immediate results, one may benefit from practicing visualization. One may practice creating images that help develop the chakras or visualize blissful pictures of communion with living nature, etc. But only those images, which are filled with exultation of happiness, harmony, joy, subtlety, and bliss, will make for one's correct spiritual development. Corresponding types of paintings, musical compositions and art photography, etc. may also serve as an aid.

Dhyana

Dhyana is the stage of meditative trainings that conducts one to Samadhi.

Meditation is work of the consciousness aimed at consciousness development on the path to Perfection, to Mergence with the Creator. Meditation is practiced at three stages of the Patanjali's scheme.

At the dharana stage, students learn, among other things, to expand the consciousness in the subtlest and the most beautiful that exists in the world of matter. By means of such attunement they establish themselves in the sattva guna.

And through working with Yidam they can immediately come in contact with a Manifestation of the Divine Consciousness and experience Samadhi.

At the dhyana stage, students work on increasing the "mass" of the consciousness and obtaining power in subtlety.

At the next stage, the stage of Samadhi, their efforts are focused on interaction of the individual consciousness with the Consciousness of the Creator and on merging with Him in His Infinity.

At the dhyana stage, meditative work is especially effective if it is performed at special *places of power* — areas on the Earth's surface that have a special energy impact on human beings. Among the variety of them only those should be chosen that make for expanding of the consciousness in the subtlest eons. A correctly selected sequence of such places ensures that the most complex tasks of correct *crystallization* (i.e. quantitative growth) of the consciousness will be solved easily and with little effort.

For the same purpose, one can meditate during athletic exercises, as well as practice winter swimming and *meditative running.*

The structure of the human organism responsible for meditation is the lower *bubble of perception* (this term was introduced by Juan Matus; see [3] for details) the principal part of which is the anahata chakra supplied with energy by the lower dantian (a complex of the three lower chakras).

From the very beginning of meditative training until the ultimate victory of Merging with the Primordial Consciousness, one must always remember that man's main merit is measured by the level of the development of the spiritual heart. This is by what man can merge initially with God. This is why it is the spiritual heart that man should develop and keep pure in every possible way. Everything said above allows us to take it not as a nice figure of speech or a metaphor, but as a quite practical knowledge and instruction.

The steps of one's spiritual ascent that we are discussing now are meant for teaching one how to position the consciousness, first, in cleansed ana-

hata, then to ensure the growth of anahata within the body and then beyond it — within the *cocoon*, then within the Earth and beyond the planet
in the highest eons.

In this way we can grow as Love. God is Love;
this is why one can merge with Him only after
becoming Great Love, a Great Soul consisting of
Love (Mahatma)!

And there are no other ways of developing Di-
vinity, except for these fundamental steps that we
are describing here.

Samadhi

This stage includes a range of the highest spiritual achievements — from the first Samadhis —
up to Mergence with the Primordial Consciousness and with the Absolute.

The consciousness of the spiritual seeker pre-
pared at the previous stage becomes capable of
getting in *contact* with the Consciousness of God
in the highest eons. These first *contacts* give one
a vivid novelty of *bliss*, which is what the term *Samadhi* denotes [3].

In contrast to Samadhi, Nirvana is a stable
Mergence with the Consciousness of God in which
the feeling of the localized "I" disappears. The term
Nirvana means "complete burning away", i.e. los-
ing the individuality through Mergence with God

in the aspects of the Holy Spirit or the Creator. And it really happens.

In the Bhagavad Gita, Krishna speaks about Samadhi and about two principal stages of Nirvana: Nirvana in Brahman (the Holy Spirit) and Nirvana in Ishvara (the Creator).

But in India, the term *Nirvana* became widely used by Buddhists at some point in time, and later on, this term along with Buddhism, was "forced out" from India by Hindus. Instead of using the term *Nirvana*, Hindu schools started to expand the meaning of the term *Samadhi* by adding to it various prefixes. Various schools used these composite words, and because of this the term *Samadhi* became "diffused" and lost its unambiguity. This is why it makes sense to get back to the accurate terminology that God introduced into spiritual culture through Krishna.

So, in order to get from Samadhi (Bliss of Contact) to Nirvana (Mergence) one has to have a large and strong consciousness, developed by preceding trainings. In addition to this, it has to be firmly established in Divine subtlety.

If these conditions are fulfilled, then all one needs to do is just to find an entrance into the required eon, to enter it, and to dissolve oneself in its Consciousness using the method of *total reciprocity*, which one has to master in advance.

This task requires not only meditative skills but ethical preparation as well: destroying the lower "I" in every possible way and replacing it with the collective we first, and then with the universal "I", i.e. with Paramatman.

This is the only way man can connect to the unlimited Divine Power.

"... We have an inexhaustible reservoir of psychic energy!" [2] (Hierarchy:394), says God.

But "if one were to expound the conditions and the aims of Yoga, the number of applicants would not be great. Terrifying for them would be the renunciation of selfhood..." [1]

In connection to the above said, I want to cite the Carlos Castaneda's book *The Power of Silence*: "... War, for a (spiritual) warrior, is the total struggle against that individual "I" that has deprived man of power." (see [3]).

... One explores the highest eons of the Absolute one after another. Before starting exploring the next eon, one has to accumulate the power of the consciousness for a long time, sometimes for years, in order to be able to enter it and remain in it. The only exception is people who approached these stages in their previous incarnations and maintained the necessary amount of *personal power* and the level of the subtlety of the consciousness.

Read about the Path to spiritual Perfection in more detail — in the books listed in the Bibliography.

Recommended literature

1. Agni Yoga. Fiery World. III. "Detskaya Litera-tura", Novosibirsk, 1991 *(in Russian)*.

2. Agni Yoga. Hierarchy. Naberezhnye Chelny, 1991 *(in Russian)*.

3. Antonov V.V. (ed.) — Classics of Spiritual Phi-losophy and the Present. "New Atlanteans", Bancroft, 2008.

4. Antonov V.V. — Ecopsychology. "New Atlante-ans", Bancroft, 2008.

5. Antonov V.V. — Forest Lectures on the High-est Yoga. "New Atlanteans", Bancroft, 2008.

6. Antonov V.V. — How God Can Be Cognized. Book 2. Autobiographies of God's Disciples. "New Atlanteans", Bancroft, 2008 *(in Russian)*. (ed.)

7. Antonov V.V. — Spiritual Heart: Path to the Cre-ator (Poems-Meditations and Revelations). "New Atlanteans", Bancroft, 2008 (in Russian). (ed.)

8. Antonov V.V. — Spiritual Work with Children. "New Atlanteans", Bancroft, 2008. (ed.)

9. Antonov V.V. — Sexology. "New Atlanteans", Bancroft, 2008.

10. Antonov V.V. — How God Can Be Cognized. Autobiography of a Scientist Who Studied God. "New Atlanteans", Bancroft, 2009.

11. Antonov V.V. — Anatomy of God. "New Atlanteans", Bancroft, 2010.

12. Antonov V.V. — Life for God. "New Atlanteans", Bancroft, 2010.

13. Antonov V.V. — Spiritual Heart. The Religion of Unity. "New Atlanteans", Bancroft, 2010.

14. Teplyy A.V. — Book of the Warrior of Spirit. "New Atlanteans", Bancroft, 2008.

15. Zubkova A.B. — Story about Princess Nesmeyana and Ivan. "New Atlanteans", Bancroft, 2007 *(in Russian)*.

16. Zubkova A.B. — Dialogues with Pythagoras. "New Atlanteans", 2008 *(in Russian)*.

17. Zubkova A.B. — Dobrynya. Byliny. "New Atlanteans", Bancroft, 2008 *(in Russian)*.

18. Zubkova A.B. — Book of the Born in the Light. Revelations of the Divine Atlanteans. "New Atlanteans", Bancroft, 2008 *(in Russian)*.

19. Zubkova A.B. — Divine Parables. "New Atlanteans", Bancroft, 2008 *(in Russian)*.

Our video films:

1. Immersion into Harmony of Nature. The Way to Paradise. (Slideshow), 90 minutes (on CD or DVD).
2. Spiritual Heart. 70 minutes (on DVD).
3. Sattva (Harmony, Purity). 60 minutes (on DVD).
4. Sattva of Mists. 75 minutes (on DVD).
5. Sattva of Spring. 90 minutes (on DVD).
6. Art of Being Happy. 42 minutes (on DVD).
7. Keys to the Secrets of Life. Achievement of Immortality. 38 minutes (on DVD).
8. Bhakti Yoga. 47 minutes (on DVD).
9. Kriya Yoga. 40 minutes (on DVD).
10. Practical Ecopsychology. 60 minutes (on DVD).
11. Yoga of Krishna. 80 minutes (on DVD).
12. Yoga of Buddhism. 135 minutes (on DVD).
13. Taoist Yoga. 91 minutes (on DVD).
14. Ashtanga Yoga. 60 minutes (on DVD).

You may order our books and films at Lulu e-store:

http://stores.lulu.com/spiritualheart

and at Amazon:

http://astore.amazon.com/spiritual-art-20

You can also download our video films, screensavers, printable calendars, etc. from the site:

www.spiritual-art.info

See on the site www.swami-center.org our books, photo gallery, and other materials in different languages.

Design —
by Maria Shtil,
Ekaterina Smirnova

Made in the USA
Coppell, TX
17 November 2022

86540414R00015